Company's Coming ®

hearty soups

Choice recipes from
Company's Coming cookbooks

Jean Paré

meatball vegetable soup

To save time, you can use cooked, frozen meatballs for this recipe. You can also cook up a double batch of these meatballs, freeze half and add to spaghetti and tomato sauce on another night.

Large egg	1	1
Dried oregano	1 tsp.	5 mL
Garlic clove, minced (or 1/4 tsp., 1 mL, powder)	1	1
Salt	1/2 tsp.	2 mL
Lean ground beef	1 lb.	454 g

Combine first 4 ingredients in large bowl.

Add beef. Mix well. Roll into 1 inch (2.5 cm) balls. Heat large non-stick frying pan on medium-high. Add meatballs. Cook for about 5 minutes, turning occasionally, until browned. Transfer to paper towels to drain.

Cooking oil	1 tsp.	5 mL
Medium onion, thinly sliced	1	1

Heat cooking oil in same frying pan on medium. Add onion. Cook for 5 to 10 minutes, stirring often, until onion is softened.

Water	6 cups	1.5 L
Thinly sliced carrot	1/2 cup	125 mL
Thinly sliced celery	1/2 cup	125 mL
Beef bouillon powder	2 tbsp.	30 mL
Chopped fresh parsley (or 3/4 tsp., 4 mL, flakes)	1 tbsp.	15 mL
Worcestershire sauce	2 tsp.	10 mL
Chopped fresh basil (or 1/2 tsp., 2 mL, dried)	1 1/2 tsp.	7 mL
Salt, sprinkle		
Pepper, sprinkle		
Parmesan cheese, for garnish		

Combine next 9 ingredients in large saucepan. Bring to a boil. Reduce heat to medium-low. Add onion and meatballs. Stir. Simmer, covered, for about 30 minutes, stirring occasionally, until carrot and celery are tender and meatballs are fully cooked.

Garnish individual servings with cheese. Makes about 8 cups (2 L).

1 cup (250 mL): 125 Calories; 5.8 g Total Fat (2.6 g Mono, trace Poly, 2.1 g Sat); 55 mg Cholesterol; 4 g Carbohydrate; 1 g Fibre; 13 g Protein; 1023 mg Sodium

hearty wild rice soup

*Earthy mushrooms and a pleasant hint of tarragon complement the nutty
flavour of wild rice. Delicious.*

Cooking oil	2 tsp.	10 mL
Chopped fresh white mushrooms	2 cups	500 mL
Lean ground beef	1 lb.	454 g
Chopped onion	1 cup	250 mL
Dried tarragon	1 tsp.	5 mL
All-purpose flour	3 tbsp.	50 mL
Prepared beef broth	6 cups	1.5 L
Wild rice	2/3 cup	150 mL
Grated carrot	1/2 cup	125 mL

Heat cooking oil in large saucepan on medium. Add next 4 ingredients.
Scramble-fry for about 10 minutes until beef is no longer pink. Drain.

Sprinkle with flour. Heat and stir for 1 minute.

Add broth and rice. Stir. Bring to a boil. Reduce heat to medium-low.
Simmer, covered, for about 50 minutes, stirring occasionally, until rice
is tender.

Add carrot. Stir. Cook, uncovered, for about 2 minutes, stirring often, until
carrot is tender-crisp. Skim any fat from surface of soup (see Tip, page 64).
Makes about 8 cups (2 L).

*1 cup (250 mL): 187 Calories; 6.6 g Total Fat (2.9 g Mono, 0.7 g Poly, 2.2 g Sat);
29 mg Cholesterol; 16 g Carbohydrate; 2 g Fibre; 15 g Protein; 646 mg Sodium*

vegetable tortellini bowl

Packed with vegetables, this light tomatoey broth becomes a meal with the addition of plump tortellini.

Cooking oil	1 tbsp.	15 mL
Chopped onion	2 cups	500 mL
Garlic cloves, minced (or 1/2 tsp., 2 mL, powder)	2	2
Prepared chicken broth	12 cups	3 L
Can of diced tomatoes, drained	14 oz.	398 mL
Chopped zucchini (with peel)	1 1/2 cups	375 mL
Grated carrot	1 1/2 cups	375 mL
Chopped yellow (or red) pepper	1 cup	250 mL
Bay leaves	2	2
Dried rosemary, crushed	1 tsp.	5 mL
Salt	1/4 tsp.	1 mL
Package of fresh beef-filled tortellini	12 1/2 oz.	350 g
Fresh spinach leaves, lightly packed	3 cups	750 mL

Heat cooking oil in Dutch oven or large pot on medium-high. Add onion. Cook, uncovered, for 5 to 10 minutes, stirring often, until onion is softened. Add garlic. Heat and stir for 1 to 2 minutes until fragrant.

Add next 8 ingredients. Stir. Bring to a boil.

Add tortellini. Stir. Reduce heat to medium. Boil gently, uncovered, for about 8 minutes, stirring occasionally, until tortellini is tender but firm.

Add spinach. Stir. Cook, uncovered, for about 2 minutes until spinach is wilted. Discard bay leaves. Makes about 15 cups (3.75 L). Serves 8.

1 serving: 235 Calories; 6.8 g Total Fat (1.1 g Mono, 0.7 g Poly, 0.9 g Sat); 15 mg Cholesterol; 36 g Carbohydrate; 3 g Fibre; 10 g Protein; 1602 mg Sodium

spicy beef and rice soup

If you can't find Mexican-style stewed tomatoes, a can of plain or Italian-style will do just as well.

Cooking oil	2 tsp.	10 mL
Beef minute (or fast-fry) steaks, cut into 1 inch (2.5 cm) cubes	1 lb.	454 g
Finely chopped onion	1/4 cup	60 mL
Garlic clove, minced (or 1/4 tsp., 1 mL, powder)	1	1
Chopped fresh basil (or 1 1/2 tsp., 7 mL, dried)	2 tbsp.	30 mL
Dried oregano	1/2 tsp.	2 mL
Salt	1/2 tsp.	2 mL
Pepper	1/8 tsp.	0.5 mL
Dried crushed chilies	1/4 tsp.	1 mL
Dried thyme	1/4 tsp.	1 mL
Water	5 cups	1.25 L
Can of Mexican-style stewed tomatoes, drained and diced	14 oz.	398 mL
Long grain white rice	1/2 cup	125 mL
Chili powder	1/4 tsp.	1 mL
Hot pepper sauce, to taste		
Chopped fresh cilantro (or parsley)	2 tbsp.	30 mL

Heat cooking oil in large frying pan on medium-high. Add next 3 ingredients. Cook for 2 to 3 minutes, stirring often, until beef is browned. Transfer to medium bowl.

Add next 6 ingredients. Stir. Cover. Set aside.

Combine next 5 ingredients in large saucepan. Bring to a boil. Reduce heat to medium-low. Simmer, covered, for about 20 minutes until rice is tender. Add beef mixture. Stir. Cook, uncovered, for about 5 minutes, stirring often, until heated through.

Add cilantro. Stir gently. Makes about 8 cups (2 L).

1 cup (250 mL): 186 Calories; 6.7 g Total Fat (2.9 g Mono, 0.6 g Poly, 2.2 g Sat); 41 mg Cholesterol; 13 g Carbohydrate; 1g Fibre; 18 g Protein; 340 mg Sodium

borscht

This "beefed up" version of borscht packs a protein punch.

Cooking oil	1 tsp.	5 mL
Extra-lean ground beef	1 lb.	454 g
Chopped onion	1 cup	250 mL
Water	5 cups	1.25 L
Chopped leek (white part only)	2 cups	500 mL
Can of diced tomatoes (with juice)	14 oz.	398 mL
Medium peeled potatoes, diced	2	2
Coarsely shredded cabbage	1 cup	250 mL
Baby carrots, sliced	6	6
Granulated sugar	1 tsp.	5 mL
Liquid gravy browner	1 tsp.	5 mL
Dried dillweed	1/2 tsp.	2 mL
Bay leaf	1	1
Cans of whole cooked beets (14 oz., 398 mL, each), with juice, grated	2	2
Beef bouillon powder	1 1/2 tbsp.	25 mL
Light sour cream	1/2 cup	125 mL
Chopped fresh chives	1 tsp.	5 mL

Heat cooking oil in Dutch oven or large pot on medium. Add beef and onion. Scramble-fry for about 10 minutes until onion is softened and beef is no longer pink.

Add next 10 ingredients. Stir. Cook, uncovered, for about 30 minutes, stirring occasionally, until vegetables are tender.

Add beets with juice and bouillon powder. Stir. Cook, uncovered, for about 5 minutes, stirring occasionally, until heated through.

Spoon sour cream and sprinkle chives onto individual servings. Makes about 14 cups (3.5 L).

1 cup (250 mL): 133 Calories; 4.1 g Total Fat (1.8 g Mono, 0.4 g Poly, 1.9 g Sat); 18 mg Cholesterol; 17 g Carbohydrate; 2 g Fibre; 8 g Protein; 437 mg Sodium

banh pho bo
(Vietnamese Beef Noodle Soup)

Ban-foh-BOH is served throughout Vietnam. Watch knives fly as Vietnamese cooks slice vegetables into thin, matchstick strips, a method called cutting julienne.

Cooking oil	1 tbsp.	15 mL
Chopped onion	1 cup	250 mL
Finely grated ginger root (or 1/2 tsp., 2 mL, ground ginger)	2 tsp.	10 mL
Garlic clove, minced (or 1/4 tsp., 1 mL, powder)	1	1
Coarsely ground pepper, sprinkle		
Ground cinnamon, sprinkle		
Water	3 cups	750 mL
Cans of condensed chicken broth (10 oz., 284 mL, each)	2	2
Grated carrot	1/2 cup	125 mL
Beef bouillon powder	2 tsp.	10 mL
Fresh hot chili pepper, finely diced (see Tip, page 64)	1	1
Beef tenderloin steak, very thinly sliced across the grain (see Tip, page 64)	5 oz.	140 g
Fresh bean sprouts	1/3 cup	75 mL
Green onions, cut into 1 1/2 inch (3.8 cm) pieces and then cut julienne	2	2

Fish sauce	3 tbsp.	50 mL
Lime juice	1 tbsp.	15 mL
Package of small rice stick noodles	8 oz.	225 g
Boiling water, to cover		
Finely shredded basil (or cilantro), for garnish		

Heat cooking oil in large saucepan on medium-high. Add onion. Cook, uncovered, for 5 to 10 minutes, stirring often, until softened.

Add next 4 ingredients. Heat and stir for 1 to 2 minutes until fragrant.

Add next 5 ingredients. Stir. Bring to a boil. Reduce heat to medium-low. Simmer, covered, for 10 minutes.

Add next 5 ingredients. Stir. Bring to a boil on medium-low. Turn off heat. Let stand, covered, until beef is cooked to desired doneness. Makes about 7 cups (1.75 L).

Cover noodles with boiling water in large heatproof bowl. Let stand for about 3 minutes until softened. Drain. Divide noodles among 6 large soup bowls. Ladle soup over top.

Garnish individual servings with basil. Serves 6.

1 serving: 258 Calories; 5.1 g Total Fat (2.5 g Mono, 1.1 g Poly, 1.1 g Sat); 10 mg Cholesterol; 41 g Carbohydrate; 2 g Fibre; 12 g Protein; 1757 mg Sodium

hearty chicken soup

Chunky vegetables, chicken and chickpeas make this a filling slow-cooker meal. To have this waiting for you when you walk in the door, prepare and refrigerate everything the night before. Just remember to chill the chopped chicken separately and brown it immediately before adding to the stockpot in the morning.

Prepared chicken broth	6 cups	1.5 L
Can of chickpeas (garbanzo beans), rinsed and drained	14 oz.	398 mL
Chopped onion	1 1/2 cups	375 mL
Roma (plum) tomatoes, seeds removed, chopped	3	3
Chopped carrot	1/2 cup	125 mL
Chopped celery	1/2 cup	125 mL
Tomato paste (see Tip, page 64)	1/4 cup	60 mL
Bay leaf	1	1
Pepper	1/2 tsp.	2 mL
Cooking oil	2 tsp.	10 mL
Boneless, skinless chicken thighs, chopped	1 lb.	454 g
Chopped fresh parsley (or 1 1/2 tsp., 7 mL, flakes), optional	2 tbsp.	30 mL

Combine first 9 ingredients in 3 1/2 to 4 quart (3.5 to 4 L) slow cooker.

Heat cooking oil in large frying pan on medium. Add chicken. Cook for 5 to 10 minutes, stirring occasionally, until browned. Add to slow cooker. Stir. Cook, covered, on Low for 8 to 10 hours or on High for 4 to 5 hours. Discard bay leaf.

Add parsley. Stir well. Makes about 11 cups (2.75 L).

1 cup (250 mL): *145 Calories; 4.8 g Total Fat (1.7 g Mono, 1.3 g Poly, 1 g Sat); 37 mg Cholesterol; 12 g Carbohydrate; 2 g Fibre; 14 g Protein; 511 mg Sodium*

turkey and bacon chowder

A delicious, healthy soup that's easy on the waistline!

Bacon slices, diced	5	5
Lean ground turkey	1/2 lb.	225 g
Sliced fresh white mushrooms	2 1/2 cups	625 mL
Chopped celery	1/2 cup	125 mL
Chopped onion	1/2 cup	125 mL
Diced red pepper	1/4 cup	60 mL
Finely chopped green onion	1/4 cup	60 mL
Turkey stock (or prepared chicken broth)	5 cups	1.25 L
Chopped unpeeled red potato	3 cups	750 mL
Dried thyme	1/2 tsp.	2 mL
Salt	1/2 tsp.	2 mL
Pepper	1/4 tsp.	1 mL
Frozen kernel corn	1/2 cup	125 mL
All-purpose flour	1/4 cup	60 mL
Dijon mustard	1 tbsp.	15 mL
Skim evaporated milk	3/4 cup	175 mL

Cook bacon in large saucepan on medium until crisp. Transfer with slotted spoon to paper towels to drain. Set aside.

Heat 1 tbsp. (15 mL) drippings in same saucepan on medium. Add turkey. Scramble-fry for about 5 minutes until no longer pink.

Add next 5 ingredients. Stir. Cook for about 5 minutes, stirring often, until vegetables are softened.

Add next 5 ingredients. Stir. Bring to a boil. Reduce heat to medium-low. Simmer, covered, for 15 to 20 minutes, stirring occasionally, until potato is tender.

Add corn and bacon. Stir.

Combine flour and mustard in small bowl. Stir in evaporated milk until smooth. Slowly stir into soup. Heat and stir on medium for about 5 minutes until boiling and slightly thickened. Makes about 9 cups (2.25 L).

1 cup (250 mL): 172 Calories; 6.0 g Total Fat (2.3 g Mono, 1.1 g Poly, 2.1 g Sat); 25 mg Cholesterol; 20 g Carbohydrate; 2 g Fibre; 11 g Protein; 749 mg Sodium

cheddar chicken soup

Serve this lovely orange soup with some herbed biscuits and apple slices for a well-rounded supper.

Water	2 1/2 cups	625 mL
Grated carrot	3/4 cup	175 mL
Grated peeled potato	1/2 cup	125 mL
Finely diced celery	1/4 cup	60 mL
Finely diced onion	1/4 cup	60 mL
Chicken bouillon powder	1 tbsp.	15 mL
Diced cooked chicken	2 cups	500 mL
Milk	1 cup	250 mL
Steak sauce	1 tsp.	5 mL
All-purpose flour	1/4 cup	60 mL
Salt	1/2 tsp.	2 mL
Pepper	1/8 tsp.	0.5 mL
Milk	1/2 cup	125 mL
Grated sharp Cheddar cheese	2 cups	500 mL

Sour cream, for garnish
Chopped fresh chives, for garnish

Combine first 6 ingredients in large saucepan. Bring to a boil. Reduce heat to medium-low. Simmer, uncovered, for about 5 minutes until vegetables are tender.

Add next 3 ingredients. Stir. Bring to a boil. Reduce heat to medium.

Combine next 3 ingredients in small bowl. Stir in second amount of milk until smooth. Slowly stir into vegetable mixture until boiling and slightly thickened.

Add cheese. Heat and stir on medium-low until melted. Do not boil.

Garnish individual servings with sour cream and chives. Makes about 6 1/2 cups (1.6 L).

1 cup (250 mL): *281 Calories; 14.1 g Total Fat (4.1 g Mono, 0.7 g Poly, 8.5 g Sat); 80 mg Cholesterol; 12 g Carbohydrate; 1 g Fibre; 26 g Protein; 762 mg Sodium*

pastry-topped chicken chowder

The delicious, flaky covering is sure to impress. Remember that puff pastry needs to be cold to roll easily. Wrap it in plastic if you're not using it immediately.

Cooking oil	2 tsp.	10 mL
Boneless, skinless chicken breast halves, cut into 1/2 inch (12 mm) cubes	6 oz.	170 g
Chopped fresh white mushrooms	1 cup	250 mL
Diced peeled potato	1 cup	250 mL
Garlic cloves, minced (or 1/2 tsp., 2 mL, powder)	2	2
Salt	1/2 tsp.	2 mL
Pepper	1/2 tsp.	2 mL
Dried crushed chilies	1/4 tsp.	1 mL
All-purpose flour	1 tbsp.	15 mL
Tomato paste (see Tip, page 64)	1 tbsp.	15 mL
Dried tarragon	1/2 tsp.	2 mL
Prepared chicken broth	2 1/2 cups	625 mL
Sun-dried tomatoes in oil, blotted dry, chopped	1/3 cup	75 mL
Balsamic vinegar	2 tbsp.	30 mL
Whipping cream	1/2 cup	125 mL
Chopped green onion	1/3 cup	75 mL
Package of puff pastry (14 oz., 397 g), thawed according to package directions	1/2	1/2
Large egg, fork-beaten	1	1

Heat cooking oil in large saucepan on medium. Add chicken. Cook, uncovered, for about 5 minutes, stirring occasionally, until no longer pink inside.

Add next 6 ingredients. Cook for about 5 minutes, stirring occasionally, until mushrooms release liquid.

Add next 3 ingredients. Heat and stir for 1 minute.

Add next 3 ingredients. Heat and stir until boiling. Reduce heat to medium-low. Simmer, covered, for 15 to 20 minutes, stirring occasionally, until potato is tender.

Add whipping cream and green onion. Stir. Makes about 5 cups (1.25 L). Ladle into six 1 cup (250 mL) ovenproof ramekins. Place on baking sheet with sides. Set aside.

Roll out puff pastry on lightly floured surface to 10 x 15 inch (25 cm x 37 cm) rectangle. Cut into six 5 inch (12.5 cm) squares.

Brush top rims of ramekins with egg. Place 1 pastry square over each ramekin. Press pastry to ramekins to seal. Gently brush egg on pastry. Bake in 400°F (205°C) oven for about 20 minutes until pastry is puffed and golden. Serves 6.

1 serving: 360 Calories; 23.4 g Total Fat (6.8 g Mono, 8.3 g Poly, 6.8 g Sat); 77 mg Cholesterol; 26 g Carbohydrate; 1 g Fibre; 13 g Protein; 695 mg Sodium

thai-style pork soup

Spicy curry heats up this hearty soup. Serve with some take-out spring rolls for a meal with Asian flair.

Cooking oil	1 tbsp.	15 mL
Pork tenderloin, trimmed of fat and cut into thin strips (see Tip, page 64)	1/2 lb.	225 g
Red curry paste	1 tbsp.	15 mL
Low-sodium prepared chicken broth	4 cups	1 L
Can of cut baby corn, drained	14 oz.	398 mL
Thinly sliced red pepper	1 cup	250 mL
Brown sugar, packed	1 tsp.	5 mL
Fish sauce	1 tsp.	5 mL
Fresh spinach leaves, lightly packed	2 cups	500 mL
Finely shredded basil (or 1 1/2 tsp., 7 mL, dried)	2 tbsp.	30 mL
Lime juice	1 tbsp.	15 mL

Heat cooking oil in large saucepan on medium-high. Add pork. Cook, uncovered, for about 5 minutes, stirring occasionally, until browned. Transfer to small bowl. Cover to keep warm.

Add curry paste to same saucepan. Heat and stir on medium for about 1 minute until fragrant.

Add next 5 ingredients. Stir. Bring to a boil. Reduce heat to medium-low. Simmer, covered, for about 5 minutes until red pepper is tender-crisp.

Add spinach and pork. Stir. Simmer, uncovered, for about 2 minutes, stirring occasionally, until pork is heated through and spinach is wilted.

Add basil and lime juice. Stir. Makes about 6 cups (1.5 L). Serves 4.

1 serving: 199 Calories; 7.7 g Total Fat (3.9 g Mono, 1.8 g Poly, 1.2 g Sat); 35 mg Cholesterol; 17 g Carbohydrate; 3 g Fibre; 18 g Protein; 907 mg Sodium

krautfurter chowder

Long after Oktoberfest is but a memory, this mellow blend of flavours will have even those who aren't sauerkraut fans asking for seconds.

Hard margarine (or butter)	1 tbsp.	15 mL
Medium onion, very thinly sliced	1	1
Sauerkraut, drained	2 cups	500 mL
Water	5 cups	1.25 L
Frozen hash brown potatoes	3 cups	750 mL
Frozen mixed vegetables	1 1/2 cups	375 mL
Chicken bouillon powder	1 1/2 tbsp.	25 mL
European wieners, sliced	5	5
Ground rosemary	1/4 tsp.	1 mL
Pepper	1/8 tsp.	0.5 mL

Melt margarine in large saucepan on medium. Add onion. Cook, uncovered, for about 5 minutes, stirring often, until onion is softened. Add sauerkraut. Cook, uncovered, for 3 to 4 minutes, stirring often, until heated through.

Add next 4 ingredients. Stir. Cook, uncovered, on low for about 5 minutes, stirring occasionally, until vegetables are tender.

Add remaining 3 ingredients. Stir. Cook, uncovered, for about 5 minutes, stirring often, until heated through. Makes about 9 2/3 cups (2.4 L).

1 cup (250 mL): 182 Calories; 8.8 g Total Fat (4.1 g Mono, 1.1 g Poly, 3.0 g Sat); 15 mg Cholesterol; 20 g Carbohydrate; 3 g Fibre; 6 g Protein; 892 mg Sodium

smoked pork and vegetable soup

Put this slow-simmering soup on the stove after supper. Before you turn in for the night, remove the tender meat from the bones and refrigerate. The next evening, just skim off the fat, heat and serve with breadsticks or crusty rolls.

Cooking oil	2 tbsp.	30 mL
Finely chopped onion	1 1/2 cups	375 mL
Finely chopped carrot	1 cup	250 mL
Finely chopped yellow turnip	1 cup	250 mL
Finely chopped celery	1/2 cup	125 mL
Garlic cloves, minced (or 1 tsp., 5 mL, powder)	4	4
Prepared chicken broth	8 cups	2 L
Smoked pork hocks (or meaty ham bone)	2 1/4 lbs.	1 kg
Can of diced tomatoes (with juice)	28 oz.	796 mL
Yellow split peas, rinsed and drained	3/4 cup	175 mL
Dry (or alcohol-free) red wine	1/3 cup	75 mL
Tomato paste (see Tip, page 64)	1/4 cup	60 mL
Bay leaves	2	2

Diced ham, for garnish
Chopped fresh parsley, for garnish

Heat cooking oil in Dutch oven or large pot on medium. Add next 4 ingredients. Stir. Cook, uncovered, for 5 to 10 minutes, stirring often, until onion is softened. Add garlic. Heat and stir for 1 to 2 minutes until fragrant.

Add next 7 ingredients. Stir. Bring to a boil. Reduce heat to medium-low. Simmer, covered, for about 2 hours, stirring occasionally, until pork starts to fall off bones. Remove from heat. Remove hocks to cutting board using slotted spoon. Remove pork from bones. Discard bones. Chop pork coarsely. Add to soup. Chill, covered, for at least 6 hours or overnight. Skim fat from soup (see Tip, page 64). Cook, uncovered, on medium for 10 to 15 minutes, stirring occasionally, until hot. Discard bay leaves.

Garnish individual servings with ham and parsley. Makes about 12 1/2 cups (3.1 L).

1 cup (250 mL): *304 Calories; 17.1 g Total Fat (8.1 g Mono, 2.5 g Poly, 5.1 g Sat); 77 mg Cholesterol; 18 g Carbohydrate; 2 g Fibre; 19 g Protein; 1498 mg Sodium*

minestrone and pesto

Mama mia! So much flavour in one bowl!

Italian sausages, casings removed	4	4
Olive (or cooking) oil	1 tbsp.	15 mL
Chopped green pepper	1 cup	250 mL
Chopped leek (white part only)	1 cup	250 mL
Chopped celery	1/2 cup	125 mL
Garlic cloves, minced (or 1/2 tsp., 2 mL, powder)	2	2
Prepared chicken broth	6 cups	1.5 L
Medium tomatoes, peeled (see Tip, page 64) and chopped	6	6
Tiny pasta (such as orzo or alphabet)	1/2 cup	125 mL
Granulated sugar	1 tsp.	5 mL
Salt	1/4 tsp.	1 mL
Coarsely ground pepper (or 1/8 tsp., 0.5 mL, pepper)	1/4 tsp.	1 mL
Fresh spinach leaves, lightly packed, coarsely cut	2 cups	500 mL
Chopped fresh green beans	1 1/2 cups	375 mL
Frozen peas	1 cup	250 mL

PESTO

Fresh basil, packed	1/2 cup	125 mL
Grated Parmesan cheese	1/4 cup	60 mL
Pecans, toasted (see Tip, page 64)	1/4 cup	60 mL
Balsamic vinegar	2 tsp.	10 mL
Garlic clove (or 1/4 tsp., 1 mL, powder)	1	1
Olive (or cooking) oil	3 tbsp.	50 mL
Grated Parmesan cheese, for garnish		

Cook sausages in medium frying pan on medium for 15 to 20 minutes, turning occasionally, until fully cooked. Chop into 1/3 inch (1 cm) pieces. Set aside.

Heat olive oil in Dutch oven or large pot on medium-low. Add next 3 ingredients. Cook, uncovered, for 5 to 10 minutes, stirring occasionally, until leek is tender. Add garlic. Heat and stir for 1 to 2 minutes until fragrant.

Add next 6 ingredients and sausage. Stir. Bring to a boil. Reduce heat to medium-low. Simmer, uncovered, for 20 minutes, stirring occasionally.

Add next 3 ingredients. Stir. Cook, uncovered, for 5 to 7 minutes, stirring often, until beans are tender-crisp. Makes about 12 cups (3 L).

Pesto: Process first 5 ingredients in blender or food processor until smooth.

With motor running, add olive oil in thin stream through hole in lid or feed chute until well combined. Makes about 1/2 cup (125 mL) pesto. Add about 1 tbsp. (15 mL) to individual servings of soup. Stir.

Sprinkle with second amount of cheese. Serves 12.

1 serving: 242 Calories; 14 g Total Fat (7.7 g Mono, 1.9 g Poly, 3.5 g Sat); 19 mg Cholesterol; 18 g Carbohydrate; 2 g Fibre; 12 g Protein; 732 mg Sodium

easy cioppino

Pronounced chuh-PEE-noh, this Italian-sounding dish is actually a San Francisco fisherman's feast! Remember that when using fresh mussels, you must discard any that won't close before cooking, as well as any that don't open during cooking.

Mussels	1 lb.	454 g
Olive (or cooking) oil	3 tbsp.	50 mL
Garlic cloves, minced	2	2
Diced green pepper	3/4 cup	175 mL
Diced onion	3/4 cup	175 mL
Diced celery	1/4 cup	60 mL
Bay leaf	1	1
Dried oregano	1/2 tsp.	2 mL
Salt	1/2 tsp.	2 mL
Pepper	1/4 tsp.	1 mL
Fennel seed	1/4 tsp.	1 mL
Dry (or alcohol-free) white wine	3/4 cup	175 mL
Worcestershire sauce	1 tbsp.	15 mL
Clam tomato beverage (or clam juice)	2 cups	500 mL
Can of diced tomatoes (with juice)	14 oz.	398 mL
Water	1/2 cup	125 mL
Granulated sugar	2 tsp.	10 mL
Package of frozen mixed seafood, thawed	12 oz.	340 g
Cod fillets (or other white fish), any small bones removed, cut into 1 inch (2.5 cm) cubes	1/2 lb.	225 g
Lemon juice	1 tbsp.	15 mL
Chopped fresh basil	2 tbsp.	30 mL
Chopped fresh parsley	2 tbsp.	30 mL

Put mussels into medium bowl. Lightly tap to close any that are opened 1/4 inch (6 mm) or more. Discard any that do not close. Set aside.

Heat olive oil in large saucepan on medium. Add garlic. Heat and stir for 1 to 2 minutes until fragrant.

Add next 8 ingredients. Stir. Cook, uncovered, for about 5 minutes, stirring often, until vegetables start to soften.

Add wine and Worcestershire sauce. Stir. Bring to a boil. Reduce heat to medium. Boil gently, uncovered, for about 5 minutes until liquid is reduced by half.

Add next 4 ingredients. Stir. Bring to a boil.

Add next 3 ingredients and mussels. Stir. Reduce heat to medium. Boil gently, covered, for about 4 minutes until mussels are opened and fish flakes easily when tested with fork. Discard bay leaf and any unopened mussels.

Add basil and parsley. Stir. Makes about 9 cups (2.25 L).

1 cup (250 mL): 188 Calories; 6.2 g Total Fat (3.6 g Mono, 0.9 g Poly, 0.9 g Sat); 62 mg Cholesterol; 14 g Carbohydrate; 1 g Fibre; 16 g Protein; 602 mg Sodium

coconut shrimp soup

This Thai-influenced soup is sure to warm you up in more ways than one! Alter the curry paste to suit your taste for heat.

Cooking oil	2 tsp.	10 mL
Green curry paste	1 tbsp.	15 mL
Finely grated ginger root	2 tsp.	10 mL
Garlic cloves, minced (or 1/2 tsp., 2 mL, powder)	2	2
Cans of light coconut milk (14 oz., 398 mL, each)	2	2
Prepared chicken broth	1 cup	250 mL
Snow peas, trimmed and thinly sliced lengthwise	4 oz.	113 g
Stalk of lemon grass, halved	1	1
Brown sugar, packed	2 tsp.	10 mL
Fish sauce	2 tsp.	10 mL
Frozen, uncooked medium shrimp (peeled and deveined), thawed	1 lb.	454 g
Chopped fresh basil (or 2 1/4 tsp., 11 mL, dried)	3 tbsp.	50 mL
Chopped fresh cilantro (or parsley)	3 tbsp.	50 mL

Heat cooking oil in large saucepan on medium-high. Add next 3 ingredients. Heat and stir for 1 to 2 minutes until fragrant.

Add next 6 ingredients. Stir. Bring to a boil. Reduce heat to medium. Boil gently, covered, for 2 minutes to blend flavours.

Add remaining 3 ingredients. Stir. Reduce heat to medium-low. Cook, uncovered, for 3 to 5 minutes, stirring often, until shrimp turn pink. Discard lemon grass. Makes about 6 cups (1.5 L).

1 cup (250 mL): *254 Calories; 15.9 g Total Fat (1.7 g Mono, 1.3 g Poly, 11.0 g Sat); 115 mg Cholesterol; 9 g Carbohydrate; trace Fibre; 20 g Protein; 384 mg Sodium*

fish chowder

Adding a simple tossed salad makes this a fast, easy supper.

Cod fillets, any small bones removed, cut into 1 inch (2.5 cm) cubes	1 lb.	454 g
Boiling water	2 cups	500 mL
Diced peeled potato	3 cups	750 mL
Salt	1 1/2 tsp.	7 mL
Pepper	1/4 tsp.	1 mL
Bacon slices, diced	4	4
Chopped onion	1 1/2 cups	375 mL
All-purpose flour	1 tbsp.	15 mL
Can of skim evaporated milk	13 1/2 oz.	385 mL
Milk	1 cup	250 mL

Fish-shaped crackers, for garnish

Place fish in large saucepan. Add boiling water. Bring to a boil. Reduce heat to medium-low. Simmer, uncovered, until fish flakes easily when tested with fork. Do not drain. Transfer fish with slotted spoon to large plate. Flake, removing any additional bones.

Add next 3 ingredients to fish broth in same saucepan. Stir. Cook, uncovered, for 10 to 15 minutes until potato is tender. Do not drain. Coarsely mash potato in saucepan.

Cook bacon in medium frying pan on medium until almost crisp. Add onion. Stir. Cook for 5 to 10 minutes, stirring often, until bacon is crisp and onion is softened.

Sprinkle with flour. Heat and stir for 1 minute.

Slowly stir in evaporated milk and milk. Heat and stir, scraping any brown bits from bottom of pan, until boiling and thickened. Add to potato mixture. Add fish. Heat and stir for about 5 minutes until heated through.

Garnish individual servings with crackers. Makes about 8 cups (2 L).

1 cup (250 mL): 214 Calories; 6 g Total Fat (3.8 g Mono, 1.1 g Poly, 3.3 g Sat); 32 mg Cholesterol; 22 g Carbohydrate; 1 g Fibre; 18 g Protein; 636 mg Sodium

artichoke shrimp soup

Entertaining tonight? Round out this creamy, easy-to-prepare soup with a salad and some fresh baguettes for dunking. A bottle of wine and a deli dessert is all you need to finish off the menu.

Hard margarine (or butter)	1 tbsp.	15 mL
Finely chopped onion	1/4 cup	60 mL
Can of artichoke hearts, drained and chopped	14 oz.	398 mL
Garlic cloves, minced (or 1/2 tsp., 2 mL powder)	2	2
Low-sodium prepared chicken broth	1 1/2 cups	375 mL
Can of condensed cream of celery soup	10 oz.	284 mL
Frozen, cooked shrimp (peeled and deveined), thawed and chopped	4 1/2 oz.	127 g
Half-and-half cream	1/2 cup	125 mL
Chopped fresh basil	1 tbsp.	15 mL

Melt margarine in large saucepan on medium. Add onion. Cook, uncovered, for about 5 minutes, stirring often, until onion is softened.

Add artichoke hearts and garlic. Heat and stir for 1 to 2 minutes until garlic is fragrant.

Add broth and soup. Stir. Cook, uncovered, for about 10 minutes, stirring occasionally, until heated through.

Add shrimp and cream. Heat and stir for about 1 minute until heated through. Transfer to serving bowl.

Sprinkle with basil. Makes about 4 1/2 cups (1.1 L). Serves 4.

1 serving: 195 Calories; 10 g Total Fat (3.7 g Mono, 2.1 g Poly, 3.6 g Sat); 93 mg Cholesterol; 14 g Carbohydrate; 3 g Fibre; 13 g Protein; 1120 mg Sodium

manhattan clam chowder

Maybe it was those skinny New York models that inspired this tomato-based chowder, a variation of the richer, cream-based New England version.

Bacon slices, diced	3	3
Finely chopped onion	1 cup	250 mL
Finely diced celery	1 cup	250 mL
Water	3 cups	750 mL
Diced potato	2 cups	500 mL
Can of diced tomatoes (with juice)	14 oz.	398 mL
Diced carrot	1 cup	250 mL
Reserved clam liquid	1/2 cup	125 mL
Parsley flakes	2 tsp.	10 mL
Salt	3/4 tsp.	4 mL
Pepper	1/8 tsp.	0.5 mL
Ground marjoram	1/2 tsp.	2 mL
Ground thyme	1/4 tsp.	1 mL
Water	2 tbsp.	30 mL
Cornstarch	2 tbsp.	30 mL
Cans of whole baby clams (5 oz., 142 g, each), drained and liquid reserved	2	2

Cook bacon in large saucepan on medium until almost crisp. Drain all but 2 tsp. (10 mL) drippings. Add onion and celery. Cook for 5 to 10 minutes, stirring often, until onion is softened.

Add next 10 ingredients. Stir. Cook, covered, for 10 to 15 minutes until potato and carrot are tender.

Stir water into cornstarch in small cup until smooth. Slowly add to soup, stirring constantly, until boiling and thickened.

Add clams. Stir. Cook, uncovered, for about 10 minutes, stirring occasionally, until heated through. Makes about 8 cups (2 L).

1 cup (250 mL): 112 Calories; 1.9 g Total Fat (0.6 g Mono, 0.4 g Poly, 0.5 g Sat); 17 mg Cholesterol; 16 g Carbohydrate; 2 g Fibre; 8 g Protein; 428 mg Sodium

spicy sweet potato soup

A lovely autumn soup with corn and sweet potato. For more of a kick and extra colour on the garnish, add another dash of cayenne to the sour cream.

Hard margarine (or butter)	2 tbsp.	30 mL
Thinly sliced onion	2 cups	500 mL
Garlic cloves, minced	4	4
Paprika	2 tsp.	10 mL
Ground coriander	1 tsp.	5 mL
Cayenne pepper	1/4 tsp.	1 mL
Fresh peeled sweet potatoes, cut into 1 1/2 inch (3.8 cm) cubes	2 lbs.	900 g
Prepared chicken broth	8 cups	2 L
Can of cream-style corn	14 oz.	398 mL
Pepper, sprinkle		

Sour cream, for garnish
Chopped fresh chives, for garnish

Melt margarine in large saucepan on medium. Add onion. Cook, uncovered, for 5 to 10 minutes, stirring often, until softened.

Add next 4 ingredients. Heat and stir for 1 to 2 minutes until fragrant.

Add sweet potato. Toss until coated.

Add broth. Stir. Bring to a boil. Reduce heat to medium-low. Simmer, covered, for 25 to 30 minutes, stirring occasionally, until sweet potato is tender. Remove from heat. Let stand for 5 minutes. Carefully process with hand blender or in blender until smooth (see Safety Tip).

Add corn and pepper. Stir. Cook on medium-high for 3 to 4 minutes, stirring occasionally, until heated through.

Garnish individual servings with sour cream and chives. Makes about 8 cups (2 L).

1 cup (250 mL): 243 Calories; 5 g Total Fat (2.6 g Mono, 0.8 g Poly, 1.1 g Sat); 0 mg Cholesterol; 43 g Carbohydrate; 6 g Fibre; 8 g Protein; 1018 mg Sodium

Safety Tip: Follow manufacturer's instructions for processing hot liquids.

cheesy vegetable chowder

A tasty pairing of cheese and vegetables. Youngsters in the house may prefer their soup without the sherry; just stir 2 tsp. (10 mL) into each adult bowl before adding the garnish.

Hard margarine (or butter)	3 tbsp.	50 mL
Chopped onion	1/3 cup	75 mL
Chopped celery	1 tbsp.	15 mL
All-purpose flour	2 tbsp.	30 mL
Chicken bouillon powder	2 tsp.	10 mL
Dry mustard	1 tsp.	5 mL
Pepper	1/8 tsp.	0.5 mL
Milk	2 cups	500 mL
Water	2 cups	500 mL
Frozen mixed vegetables, cooked	2 cups	500 mL
Process cheese loaf, cut up	1 lb.	500 g
Dry sherry (optional)	1/4 cup	60 mL

Grated medium Cheddar cheese,
     for garnish
Chopped fresh chives, for garnish

Melt margarine in large saucepan on medium. Add onion and celery. Cook, uncovered, for about 5 minutes, stirring often, until onion is softened.

Add next 4 ingredients. Heat and stir for 1 minute.

Add milk and water. Heat and stir until boiling and thickened.

Add vegetables and cheese loaf. Heat and stir until cheese is melted.

Add sherry. Stir.

Garnish individual servings with Cheddar cheese and chives. Makes about 6 cups (1.5 L).

1 cup (250 mL): 423 Calories; 30.9 g Total Fat (11.0 g Mono, 1.5 g Poly, 16.8 g Sat); 75 mg Cholesterol; 14 g Carbohydrate; trace Fibre; 21 g Protein; 1566 mg Sodium

french onion soup

This soup has delicious caramelized onions and a definite herb undertone. Remind everyone—the bowls are hot!

Hard margarine (or butter)	2 tbsp.	30 mL
Medium onions, thinly sliced	8	8
Salt	1 tsp.	5 mL
Garlic cloves, minced (or 1 tsp., 5 mL, powder)	4	4
Coarsely ground pepper (or 1/4 tsp., 1 mL, pepper)	1/2 tsp.	2 mL
Dry sherry	1/2 cup	125 mL
Prepared beef broth	4 cups	1 L
Bay leaves	3	3
Sprigs of fresh thyme	3	3
Multi-grain rye bread slices, about 1/3 inch (1 cm) thick and lightly toasted or air-dried	8	8
Grated Gruyère cheese	1 1/3 cups	325 mL

Melt margarine in large saucepan on medium-low. Add onion and salt. Stir. Cook, covered, for about 45 minutes, stirring occasionally, until onion is softened but still white.

Add garlic and pepper. Stir. Cook, uncovered, on medium-high, for 5 to 10 minutes, stirring often, until onion is caramelized.

Add sherry. Heat and stir, scraping any brown bits from bottom of pan until combined.

Add next 3 ingredients. Bring to a boil. Reduce heat to medium-low. Simmer, covered, for 30 minutes, without stirring. Discard bay leaves and thyme sprigs. Makes about 5 cups (1.25 L).

Arrange 4 ovenproof bowls on baking sheet with sides. Place 2 slices of toast in each bowl. Ladle soup over bread. Let stand for 1 to 2 minutes to soak.

Sprinkle with cheese. Broil on centre rack in oven for 3 to 5 minutes until cheese is melted and golden. Let stand for 5 minutes. Carefully transfer hot soup bowls to plates. Serves 4.

1 serving: 503 Calories; 21.1 g Total Fat (8.7 g Mono, 1.9 g Poly, 9.1 g Sat); 42 mg Cholesterol; 52 g Carbohydrate; 8 g Fibre; 22 g Protein; 1964 mg Sodium

acorn squash soup

Butter gives this autumn soup its well-rounded flavour. Make sure you don't break up the bay leaf as you're stirring; you want to pull the whole leaf from the soup when it's done.

Butter	1/4 cup	60 mL
Acorn squash, peeled and cubed	1 1/2 lbs.	680 g
Chopped onion	1/2 cup	125 mL
Garlic cloves, minced (or 3/4 tsp., 4 mL, powder)	3	3
Bay leaf	1	1
Salt	1/2 tsp.	2 mL
Pepper	1/8 tsp.	0.5 mL
Water	2 cups	500 mL
Can of evaporated milk	13 1/2 oz.	385 mL

Chopped fresh chives (or green onion),
for garnish

Melt butter in large saucepan on medium. Add next 6 ingredients. Cook, uncovered, for about 5 minutes, stirring often, until onion is softened.

Add water and evaporated milk. Stir. Bring to a boil. Reduce heat to medium-low. Simmer, covered, for about 25 minutes, stirring occasionally, until squash is very tender. Discard bay leaf. Carefully process with hand blender or in blender until smooth (see Safety Tip).

Garnish individual servings with chives. Makes about 6 cups (1.5 L).

1 cup (250 mL): 190 Calories; 8.5 g Total Fat (2.4 g Mono, 0.4 g Poly, 5.2 g Sat); 25 mg Cholesterol; 24 g Carbohydrate; 3 g Fibre; 7 g Protein; 366 mg Sodium

Safety Tip: Follow manufacturer's instructions for processing hot liquids.

minestrone

Here's a large-quantity recipe that will fill your slow cooker with a nourishing soup the whole family will enjoy. To avoid hectic mornings, combine and refrigerate the first 12 ingredients in your slow-cooker liner the night before.

Prepared chicken (or vegetable) broth	6 cups	1.5 L
Cans of diced tomatoes (with juice), 14 oz. (398 mL) each	2	2
Thinly sliced leek (white part only)	3 cups	750 mL
Can of white kidney beans, rinsed and drained	19 oz.	540 mL
Shredded cabbage, lightly packed	2 cups	500 mL
Diced carrot	1 3/4 cups	425 mL
Sliced celery	1 3/4 cups	425 mL
Garlic cloves, minced (or 1/2 tsp., 2 mL, powder)	2	2
Granulated sugar	1 tsp.	5 mL
Dried basil	1/2 tsp.	2 mL
Salt	1/2 tsp.	2 mL
Pepper	1/2 tsp.	2 mL
Diced zucchini (with peel)	1 cup	250 mL
Frozen cut green beans	1 cup	250 mL

Grated Parmesan cheese, for garnish

Combine first 12 ingredients in 5 to 7 quart (5 to 7 L) slow cooker. Cook, covered, on Low for 9 to 10 hours or on High for 4 1/2 to 5 hours.

Add zucchini and green beans. Stir. Cook, covered, on High for about 20 minutes until green beans are tender.

Garnish individual servings with cheese. Makes about 15 cups (3.74 L).

1 cup (250 mL): 84 Calories; 1 g Total Fat (0.3 g Mono, 0.3 g Poly, 0.2 g Sat); 0 mg Cholesterol; 15 g Carbohydrate; 3 g Fibre; 5 g Protein; 568 mg Sodium

lemon lentil soup

A fragrant soup with a tangy, creamy broth. Pick up some pita bread or pappadums for a fast culinary visit to India.

Cooking oil	1 tbsp.	15 mL
Chopped carrot	1 1/2 cups	375 mL
Chopped onion	1 1/2 cups	375 mL
Curry powder	1 1/2 tbsp.	25 mL
Prepared vegetable (or chicken) broth	6 cups	1.5 L
Can of lentils, rinsed and drained	19 oz.	540 mL
Can of coconut milk	14 oz.	398 mL
Bay leaves	2	2
Fresh spinach leaves, lightly packed	2 cups	500 mL
Lemon juice	2 tbsp.	30 mL
Salt	1/4 tsp.	1 mL

Heat cooking oil in Dutch oven or large pot on medium-high. Add carrot and onion. Cook, uncovered, for 5 to 10 minutes, stirring often, until onion is softened.

Add curry powder. Heat and stir for 1 to 2 minutes until fragrant.

Add next 4 ingredients. Stir. Bring to a boil. Reduce heat to medium. Boil gently, covered, for about 5 minutes, stirring occasionally, until carrot is tender. Discard bay leaves.

Add remaining 3 ingredients. Heat and stir for about 2 minutes until spinach is wilted. Makes about 11 cups (2.75 L).

1 cup (250 mL): 156 Calories; 9.8 g Total Fat (1.4 g Mono, 0.7 g Poly, 6.9 g Sat); 0 mg Cholesterol; 12 g Carbohydrate; 3 g Fibre; 7 g Protein; 592 mg Sodium

bean chowder

Served with toast or fresh-baked bread, this is a quick, easy supper with a good, smoky taste.

Cooking oil	1 tbsp.	15 mL
Chopped onion	1/2 cup	125 mL
Sliced celery	1/2 cup	125 mL
Can of baked beans in tomato sauce	14 oz.	398 mL
Can of condensed tomato soup	10 oz.	284 mL
Diced summer sausage (or other spiced cooked lean sausage)	1 cup	250 mL
Milk	1 cup	250 mL
Grated peeled potato	1/2 cup	125 mL
Water	1/2 cup	125 mL
Barbecue sauce	1 tsp.	5 mL
Cayenne pepper	1/8 tsp.	0.5 mL

Heat cooking oil in large saucepan on medium-high. Add onion and celery. Cook, uncovered, for about 5 minutes, stirring often, until onion is softened.

Add remaining 8 ingredients. Stir. Reduce heat to medium-low. Simmer, uncovered, for 15 to 20 minutes, stirring occasionally, until thickened and potato is tender. Makes about 4 1/2 cups (1.1 L).

1 cup (250 mL): 319 Calories; 15.1 g Total Fat (6.6 g Mono, 2.1 g Poly, 4.9 g Sat); 27 mg Cholesterol; 36 g Carbohydrate; 9 g Fibre; 13 g Protein; 1308 mg Sodium

tomato chickpea soup

You can spice things up by using a hotter curry paste in this colourful, lemony soup. Top with dollops of plain yogurt. Ideal with a fresh loaf of crusty bread or buns.

Cooking oil	1 tbsp.	15 mL
Medium onion, chopped	1	1
Garlic cloves, minced (or 1 tsp., 5 mL, powder)	4	4
Mild curry paste	3 tbsp.	50 mL
Can of diced tomatoes (with juice)	28 oz.	796 mL
Prepared vegetable (or chicken) broth	2 cups	500 mL
Tomato paste (see Tip, page 64)	3 tbsp.	50 mL
Granulated sugar	1 tsp.	5 mL
Fresh spinach leaves, lightly packed	3 cups	750 mL
Can of chickpeas (garbanzo beans), rinsed and drained	19 oz.	540 mL
Salt, sprinkle		
Grated lemon zest	1 tsp.	5 mL

Heat cooking oil in large saucepan on medium-high. Add onion. Cook, uncovered, for about 5 minutes, stirring often, until onion is softened. Add garlic. Heat and stir for 1 to 2 minutes until fragrant.

Add curry paste. Heat and stir for about 1 minute until fragrant.

Add next 4 ingredients. Stir. Bring to a boil.

Add next 3 ingredients. Stir. Cook, uncovered, for about 2 minutes, stirring often, until spinach is wilted.

Add lemon zest. Stir. Makes about 8 cups (2 L).

1 cup (250 mL): 135 Calories; 5.2 g Total Fat (2.4 g Mono, 1.6 g Poly, 0.5 g Sat); 0 mg Cholesterol; 18 g Carbohydrate; 4 g Fibre; 6 g Protein; 464 mg Sodium

barley vegetable soup

Simply toss a dozen ingredients into a pot and simmer up some comfort food on a cold night.

Water	6 cups	1.5 L
Frozen mixed vegetables	2 cups	500 mL
Shredded cabbage	2 cups	500 mL
Sliced carrot	2 cups	500 mL
Can of condensed tomato soup	10 oz.	284 mL
Pearl barley	1/2 cup	125 mL
Beef bouillon powder	2 tbsp.	30 mL
Granulated sugar	2 tbsp.	30 mL
Dried basil	1/2 tsp.	2 mL
Salt	1/2 tsp.	2 mL
Pepper	1/2 tsp.	2 mL
Dried oregano	1/4 tsp.	1 mL

Combine all 12 ingredients in large saucepan. Bring to a boil. Reduce heat to medium-low. Simmer, covered, for about 75 minutes, stirring occasionally, until vegetables are tender. Makes about 9 cups (2.25 L).

1 cup (250 mL): 126 Calories; 1.2 g Total Fat (0.2 g Mono, 0.5 g Poly, 0.3 g Sat); trace Cholesterol; 27 g Carbohydrate; 3 g Fibre; 4 g Protein; 796 mg Sodium

lentil spinach soup

Cut this recipe in half if you haven't got a big enough pot. But serious soup-makers know you'll quickly recoup the money spent on a good stockpot by having healthy soups like this on hand.

Water	10 cups	2.5 L
Dried green lentils	2 cups	500 mL
Medium onion, chopped	1	1
Chopped celery	2/3 cups	150 mL
Chicken bouillon powder	1/4 cup	60 mL
Pepper	1/4 tsp.	1 mL
Box of frozen chopped spinach, thawed and finely chopped	10 oz.	300 g
Salt, sprinkle (optional)		

Grated medium Cheddar cheese, for garnish

Combine first 6 ingredients in Dutch oven or large pot. Cook, covered, on medium-low for about 45 minutes until lentils are soft.

Add spinach. Stir. Cook for about 5 minutes until spinach is tender. Add salt. Stir.

Garnish individual servings with cheese. Makes about 12 cups (3 L).

1 cup (250 mL): 61 Calories; 0.7 g Total Fat (0.2 g Mono, 0.3 g Poly, 0.2 g Sat); trace Cholesterol; 10 g Carbohydrate; 2 g Fibre; 5 g Protein; 676 mg Sodium

lentil and pasta soup

Tubetti is a small, tubular soup pasta ideal for this robust recipe.

Olive oil	2 tsp.	10 mL
Chopped celery	1 cup	250 mL
Finely chopped onion	1 cup	250 mL
Garlic cloves, minced	2	2
Water	7 cups	1.75 L
Can of plum tomatoes (with juice), blended	14 oz.	398 mL
Thinly sliced carrot	1 1/2 cups	375 mL
Dried green lentils	3/4 cup	175 mL
Beef (or chicken) bouillon powder	2 tbsp.	30 mL
Parsley flakes	2 tsp.	10 mL
Dried basil	1 tsp.	5 mL
Salt	1 tsp.	5 mL
Pepper, sprinkle		
Ground oregano, just a pinch		
Tubetti	1 cup	250 mL

Heat olive oil in large saucepan on medium-high. Add celery and onion. Cook, uncovered, for 5 to 10 minutes, stirring often, until onion is softened. Add garlic. Heat and stir for 1 to 2 minutes until fragrant.

Add next 10 ingredients. Stir. Bring to a boil. Reduce heat to medium-low. Simmer, partially covered, for 30 minutes.

Add tubetti. Stir. Cook, uncovered, for about 15 minutes, stirring occasionally, until pasta is tender but firm. Makes about 8 cups (2 L).

1 cup (250 mL): 158 Calories; 2 g Total Fat (1.0 g Mono, 0.4 g Poly, 0.4 g Sat); trace Cholesterol; 28 g Carbohydrate; 4 g Fibre; 8 g Protein; 893 mg Sodium

recipe index

topical tips

Chopping jalapeño peppers: Hot peppers contain capsaicin in the seeds and ribs. Removing the seeds and ribs will reduce the heat. Wear protective gloves when handling jalapeño peppers. Do not touch your face near eyes.

Peeling tomatoes: Cut an 'X' on the bottom of each tomato, just through the skin. Place tomatoes in boiling water for 30 seconds. Immediately transfer to a bowl of ice water. Let stand until cool enough to handle. Peel and discard skins.

Skimming fat: Reduce fat by placing a coffee filter on the soup's surface and blotting it up. Or allow the soup to chill in the refrigerator. The fat will harden on the surface, making it easy to lift out.

Slicing meat easily: Before cutting meat, place in freezer for about 30 minutes until just starting to freeze. If using from frozen state, partially thaw before cutting.

Toasting nuts, seeds or coconut: Cooking times will vary for each type of nut—so never toast them together. For small amounts, place ingredient in an ungreased shallow frying pan. Heat on medium for three to five minutes, stirring often, until golden. For larger amounts, spread ingredient evenly in an ungreased shallow pan. Bake in 350°F (175°C) oven for five to 10 minutes, stirring or shaking often, until golden.

Tomato paste leftovers: If a recipe calls for less than an entire can of tomato paste, freeze the unopened can for 30 minutes. Open both ends and push the contents through one end. Slice off only what you need. Freeze the remaining paste in a resealable freezer bag or plastic wrap for future use.

Nutrition Information Guidelines

Each recipe is analyzed using the Canadian Nutrient File from Health Canada, which is based on the United States Department of Agriculture (USDA) Nutrient Database.

- If more than one ingredient is listed (such as "butter or hard margarine"), or if a range is given (1 – 2 tsp., 5 – 10 mL), only the first ingredient or first amount is analyzed.

- For meat, poultry and fish, the serving size per person is based on the recommended 4 oz. (113 g) uncooked weight (without bone), which is 2 – 3 oz. (57 – 85 g) cooked weight (without bone)—approximately the size of a deck of playing cards.

- Milk used is 1% M.F. (milk fat), unless otherwise stated.

- Cooking oil used is canola oil, unless otherwise stated.

- Ingredients indicating "sprinkle," "optional" or "for garnish" are not included in the nutrition information.

- The fat in recipes and combination foods can vary greatly depending on the sources and types of fats used in each specific ingredient. For these reasons, the count of saturated, monounsaturated and polyunsaturated fats may not add up to the total fat content.